Why ...
THANK YOU!

To Amy & Kevin
Delight in what
You Write!

Here's What Others Are Saying About
"Why ... THANK YOU!"

" 'Please' may get credit for being the magic word, but a couple of other magic words are 'Thank You.' Cat Wagman shows us not only how to get our thank-you notes written, but how to have some fun along the way. Where was she when I was a kid?
Thanks for a great book, Cat. Gee, that was fun!"

Greg Howard
Creator of 'Sally Forth'

"What a terrific, fun and easy to read book! ... very essential and important to everyone from 11 to 93!!! ... I write thank-you notes all the time and I learned some new techniques from your book! I recommend it highly and will do so in my seminars!"

Andrea Nierenberg
International Sales and Motivational Consultant
President, The Nierenberg Group

"WOW! Why ... THANK YOU! will remind all of us what our parents taught us ... remember to say 'Thank you.' Your words will help smooth the way to a perfect job, better relationships, even more business for the entrepreneur."

Joe Sabah
Author of 'How to Get On Radio Talk Shows
All Across America Without Leaving Your Home or Office'

"Although little will INSPIRE folks who don't like writing thank-you notes ... your book certainly helps those who have reached that point of NOW or NEVER and have chosen 'NOW'!! ... I hope you get thank-you letters from the folks you've helped to overcome their caligratiphobia (FEAR OF WRITING THANK YOU LETTERS)."

Lynn Johnston
Creator of 'For Better or For Worse'

Why ...
THANK YOU!

*How to Have FUN
Writing
Fantastic Notes and More ...*

CAT WAGMAN

**WORKING WORDS, INC.
PEMBROKE PINES, FLORIDA**

Working Words, Inc.
2114 N. Flamingo Road, # 1114
Pembroke Pines, FL 33028-3501
www.ThankYouThankYou.com
Why ... THANK YOU!
© 1997 Catherine E. W. Wagman.
All Rights Reserved. First Edition: 1997
Printed in the United States of America.

06 05 04 03 02 01 00 99 98 97   10 9 8 7 6 5 4 3 2

ISBN: 0-9652670-4-0   printed hard cover
ISBN: 0-9652670-6-7   paperback

Library of Congress Catalog Card Number: 96-90575

Publisher's Cataloging in Publication
  (Prepared by Quality Books, Inc.)
  Wagman, Cat
    Why-- thank you! : how to have fun writing
  fantastic notes and more-- / Cat Wagman.
    p. cm.
    Includes index.

    1. Authorship--Study and teaching. 2. Creative writing--
Study and teaching. 3. Thank-you notes. 4. Etiquette. I. Title.

PN 145.W34 1997   808'.02
                                   QBI96-40268

DISCLAIMER: *This book draws on the personal experience of the author. Every effort has been
made to make this book as complete and as accurate as possible. This text should be used only as a
general guide and not as the ultimate source of business or personal etiquette. The purpose of this book
is to educate and entertain. All letters contained in this book are of the author's own composition.
The author and publisher shall have neither liability nor responsibility to any person or entity with
respect to any loss or damage caused, or alleged to be caused, directly or indirectly by the information
contained in this book.*

DEDICATION

I am dedicating this book to all who know what they want to say, but don't know how to say it or where to start.

Let Happiness and Laughter shine through your words. As you tap into your creative selves and write the feelings in your heart and soul, you will discover a new freedom of personal expression. The words will begin and continue to flow freely.

And to my husband, Jan, and my sons, Devin and Bernie, thank you for making this journey worthwhile and for confirming that "sillies" run naturally through this family.

And to the rest of my wonderful family, especially my mother and friend, Dr. Faith C. Walsh, and my cherished granddaddy, Dr. Israel J. Cramer, for their love and support of my dreams; and above all, their belief that their children can achieve anything they put their hearts and minds to.

CONTENTS

CHAPTER THREE
Let's Solve ... *"The Mystery of The Unwritten Thank-You Note"* 21

CHAPTER FOUR
"Cat's Creative Catalyst" 29

CHAPTER FIVE
What If? 35

CHAPTER SIX
WATCH OUT! Something *Fantastic* is About to Happen 37

FOREWORD

If you've ever *struggled with* or have been *intimidated by* the mere thought of putting pen to paper when writing a thank-you note, **this book is for you!** Cat Wagman has taken the fine art of saying "Thank You" to new heights with a warm and witty "quick read" that will challenge, delight, and inspire any child—*and* adult, for that matter. She shows how much fun there is in creating "from-the-heart messages" to those we care about and to those who care about us.

I know. I've taken her tips and passed them on to my grandson, Brent, who is now a First Class Thank-You Note Writer! His latest one to me included the lines,

> *"Granna, the new in-line skates you gave me*
> *for my birthday work great. I'll teach you how*
> *to use them when you visit in 3 weeks."*

Now, that will be a real struggle and a little intimidating, but with Brent's enthusiasm and some practice, I'll be skating in no time at all!

I have no doubt that once you learn the easy techniques Cat shows you, and use them when writing *your* notes, you will be delighted to find out how creative you truly are and how much fun writing can be.

ANN L. TAYLOR
1995-96 National President
Women In Communications, Inc.

PREFACE

I wrote this book for a very special person—**YOU!** As a unique individual, you have your own thoughts and feelings. To help you communicate those feelings and thoughts, I will show you, step-by-step, a professional writer's way to write a Thank-You Note in a style *all your own*.

As part of my ongoing commitment to help kids and grown-ups discover the joys of creative writing, I decided to write *"Why ...* THANK YOU!" It started with my own Thank-You Note writing experiences and grew out of a class I have taught called the *Why ...* THANK YOU! FUNshop™. I have also shared my methods with students during Career Day programs in local schools.

When my parents were kids, they *HAD* to write Thank-You Notes, and I'm sure yours did, too. However, I don't think anyone has ever approached it as something FUN to do. How many times do you think kids have heard the following?

"Did you write a Thank-You Note to Grandma, YET?!?"
or
"Just write a note and be done with it already!"

There are many books which tell you about "form and structure," but not about the actual writing of a Thank-You Note. Many grown-ups don't enjoy writing because they think it is hard to do. However, when something is FUN to do, no matter how hard or challenging it may seem, the easier and more enjoyable it becomes.

I will show you the materials you need, talk about planning, demonstrate "Cat's Creative Catalyst" and how to use it, and, of course, give a variety of Thank-You Note examples for many different occasions.

Feel free to share this book with your friends and parents. Above all, have FUN with it! Let this book help you to explore the Magical World of Words, Images, and Emotions.

Now ... have FUN and *ENJOY*!

This is my gift to you.

ACKNOWLEDGMENTS

I would like to thank the following people for their invaluable contributions during the creative, reviewing, and critiquing process ... my mother, Dr. Faith C. Walsh, as well as, my mother-in-law, Rhoda Wagman; Ann Taylor, Maryanne Schuessler Freeman, Nancy Nevin, Gail Clark Neal, Phyllis Klenetsky, Peggy Stein, Abbe Logan, Barbara Sugarman, and Adrienne Sioux Koopersmith.

I also want to thank Jerilene "Sam" Zavoda, who teaches at Pembroke Lakes Elementary in Pembroke Pines, who provided me with the opportunity to present my first *Why* ... THANK YOU! FUNshop™ in 1990.

To fellow "cat person," Paul I. Pettys of Pettys Designs Advertising, who recognized the kindred spirit and created the book cover and interior design I was looking for. To Ray Russotto for capturing the character of Moussé, our family cat, so he would have a *paw* in this book, too. Thank you to my copy editors, Julia Mullings and Ruth Kalb who fine-tuned my manuscript to perfection.

And for all of their encouragement and guidance, a special thank you to my wonderful writing and publishing mentors–R. Marilyn Schmidt of Barnegat Light Press (NJ), Dana Cassell of the Florida Freelance Writers Association, Henry Holden of Black Hawk Publishing Company (NJ), Chevy Alden of Tri-Pacer Press (FL), John Kremer of Ad-Lib Publications (IA), Betsy Lampé of Rainbow Books (FL), and many others through the Florida Publishers Association.

ABOUT THE AUTHOR

Cat Wagman, a professional writer with more than twenty-five years experience, began her communications career in Public Broadcasting. Now, as a full-time writer and consultant, she provides all types of advertising, marketing, and office procedure documentation and training materials to businesses in South Florida. She considers this her "bread-and-butter" writing, while her poetry, fantasy, and children's stories are her "dessert."

In 1976, Cat and her husband, Jan, managed to write and mail more than 150 notes in only three days—*after* they got married, and *before* they left on their honeymoon! It was from this point on that Cat became known as the family's Thank-You Note Writing Expert.

Later, Cat drew on her experiences and developed her first *Why* ... THANK YOU! FUNshop™, which she presented to her elder son's third grade class in 1990. She continues to use Thank-You Notes to introduce the joys of creative writing to kids of *all* ages (and teachers, too!) during Career Days at local schools.

As a Thank-You Note Writing Expert, Cat helps people of every age to creatively compose their thoughts and translate them to paper. Her ultimate goal is to encourage the exploration of creative writing as a recreational, therapeutic, and expressive tool for living life to the fullest. "*Why* ... THANK YOU!" grew from her love of writing, her enjoyment in teaching others, and the hundreds of Thank-You Notes she has written over the years.

INTRODUCTION

Learning and Teaching Are Lifelong Endeavors

Every day there are opportunities to learn and to teach. Everyone is a student and everyone is a teacher. Life is a school where everyone has the opportunity to be both. Each time you learn a new skill and master it, teaching that skill to someone else will come naturally.

This creative writing guide has been lovingly prepared to teach you how to compose a simple Thank-You Note. After learning the basics and putting them into practice, with each note you write, it will become easier and quicker to do.

As you master these writing techniques, you will be able to a pass your skills along and teach them to others, and perhaps, someday, to your own children and grandchildren.

This is Moussé. He is the Wagman family cat and he's the purrfect partner to help me help you have FUN!

THE GIFTS

Write Thank-You Notes for All Gifts You Receive

Throughout your lifetime, you may receive gifts for any of the following occasions:

Birthdays	Bridal Showers
Christmas	Wedding
Hanukkah	Anniversaries
Kwanzaa	Baby Showers
Bar/Bat Mitzvah	New Baby
Confirmation	New Home
Quince	Get Well
Graduations	New Job
Valentine's Day	Job Well Done
Special Trips	Promotions
Engagement	Retirement

or Just on Account of Because ...

Another wonderful reason to write Thank-You Notes is to tell those special people in your life what they mean to you. Focus on why they are important to you, all the positive things they have done for you, and what inspirations they have been. As an example, I bet you have a favorite teacher you could write to.

A gift can be absolutely anything ...

> From a box of Thank-You Note writing paper to an elegant fountain pen.
>
> Or perhaps a magazine subscription or tickets to a concert.
>
> Books.
>
> Clothes.
>
> Sporting equipment.
>
> A gift certificate or savings bond.

The list can go on and on ...

If you have a birthday coming up soon, a holiday, or any other special occasion just around the corner, a time when you may be receiving gifts—**NOW** is the time to get organized!

Helpful Hints When a Gift Arrives

1. On the back of the gift card* write a short description of what the gift is. For example: Basketball, Blue Dress, Sports Jacket. *(*No card? Then a 3" x 5" card will do!)*

2. Clip the address from the card's envelope or gift's mailing wrapper and tape the address to the back of the card. This way you won't lose it before you have a chance to put it in your address file.

3. If you don't have the address for the person who gave the gift, ASK! Especially if the person is with you at a party; or, if not, a grown-up can give it to you.

4. Always write the address in a card file** or address book *before* writing the Thank-You Note. If you have a computer, start an address file, and always remember to make a back-up disk. *(**I will show you how I set up my own card file system in Chapter 2.)*

5. If you don't have a Zip Code, call your local post office for the information.

   a. Give the exact street address, city, and state; then the clerk will be able to give the Zip Code to you.

   b. If the clerk gives a Zip+4 Code to you, be sure to write down *all* nine numbers. This nine-digit number helps to sort mail faster and the U.S. Postal Service would like everyone to use it, whenever possible.

   c. *Always ask the clerk if you may read the Zip Code back.* You want to make sure you wrote the numbers correctly, and of course,

   d. Remember to say *"Thank You!"* when you are finished getting the information.

You can look up the Zip Code yourself. Each post office usually has a Zip Code Directory available in the lobby for anyone to use.

You can also get the Zip+4 Codes off the Internet by going to: *http://www.usps.gov/ncsc/ lookups/lookup_zip+4.html* Just follow the instructions on your computer screen.

What to Do When
You Receive a TON of Gifts
(e.g., Christmas, Bar Mitzvah, Wedding, etc.)

1. Write your notes right after you receive the gift—usually "first come, first served"—particularly if you opened the gift prior to the event.

2. Put the persons to whom you are going to send Thank-You Notes in the following order:

   Priority #1
   Relatives and friends of the family who sent gifts or came to the event from out of town,

   Priority #2
   Relatives who live in the immediate area,

   Priority #3
   Friends of the family who live nearby, and

   Priority #4
   Your own friends.

Many times those who live the farthest away from you are the ones who get forgotten first when it comes time to write your Thank-You Notes to them. By giving them the highest priority, you will be sure to get those notes written first. If you aren't sure where a gift giver should be placed in the priorities, you can always ask a grown-up to help you decide.

3. Although each note will be personalized to the gift giver, certain phrases (slightly altered) may be repeated:

✱ *"I'm so glad you were able to share this joyous occasion with my family and me."*

"I'm sorry you were unable to attend ..."

Be sure to make each of these types of phrases a little bit different, just in case two or more people, who receive your Thank-You Notes, decide to share them with each other.

Sharing the Responsibility

For those grown-ups who are getting married, etc., may I suggest the following approach, which worked well for my husband and me. I wrote the Thank-You Notes to my relatives and he wrote to his, then we shared the writing of the notes to our friends.

Splitting up this long list of notes we had to write after our own wedding made a lot of sense. Each of us knew our own relatives better than the other, and we were able to personalize each note appropriately. Of course, whenever we got stuck on what to say, we would ask each other for help.

The whole process was shared and mutually experienced, and became even more fun as we worked through the pile of cards. Both my husband and I have been blessed with a good sense of humor—one of the main reasons why we married in the first place! To say the least, several notes had large doses of humor by the time we got them all done.

When Do You Write a Thank-You Note?

Try to have it written and in the mail within 48 hours of receiving the gift. The sooner you do it, the sooner you will feel a wonderful sense of accomplishment; and the sooner the person who gave you the gift will know just how special (and organized) you really are!

Write the note as soon as you can.
The same day is best, if possible.

The Right Motivation Helps

We have a rule in our house that you can't use a gift until *after* the Thank-You Note is written. For grown-ups, that also means *before* the gift is placed on a shelf, put in a drawer, or hung up in the closet. Why? Because many times, once a gift is put away, the thought about writing a Thank-You Note can be too easily forgotten. This rule helps to establish self-discipline and priorities, as well as motivation.

 CHAPTER TWO

ALWAYS BE PREPARED

Organization is the Name of the Game

Some people are *very* organized, some are not, and some are in between. By gathering the right "tools" needed **before** you start, you will automatically become quicker and more efficient. Many of these tools may be found around your house.

NOTE PAPER

You Need the Right Tools
to Do the "Write" Job!

The ten basic tools to have on hand at *all times* are:

1. **Scratch Paper:**
   Make your own supply! Save advertisement flyers, school notices, or other announcements that are printed on one side of the paper. Use the blank side as your scratch paper to write down and organize all the ideas bouncing around in your head. This method is called *brainstorming*. Once you've completed the first rough draft and made any necessary corrections to your spelling and grammar, rewrite the Thank-You Note on your good note paper.

2. **Note Paper and Envelopes:**
   Buy blank note paper or cards with envelopes in a style that you like. This stationery can be plain or have a design. There are designs that can fit almost any occasion, especially holidays, or you can choose something completely different, such as a favorite theme, sport, or hobby. If you like, you can design and make your own Thank-You Note cards. Use items you have at home, or check out your local arts and crafts store for more ideas, materials, fancy scissors with serrated edges, and copy-right-free designs published by the Dover Clip-Art Series®.

> *Whatever you do,* **PLEASE** *don't buy preprinted Thank-You Notes. They just don't say what needs to be said.*

Of course, there are cards that have "Thank You" printed on the front, which are perfectly okay, as long as they are **blank inside**. Blank cards give you enough room to write down all of your own thoughts.

Remember...
Your own message is
the most important part!

Each gift you receive is a personal selection made by a relative, friend, or associate, *just for you*. A personal Thank-You Note is your *only* way of *truly* acknowledging the time, effort, and thoughtfulness they spent choosing *your* special gift.

> **A Special Paper Note:**
> *Don't buy dark red-, blue-, or brown-colored envelopes, unless you plan to use white address labels. The sorting machines used by the U.S. Postal Service have a hard time "reading" any handwritten address information on these dark colors. You don't want your Thank-You Notes delayed or misplaced because the machine can't "see" the addresses clearly.*

3. Pens or Pencils:

Have fun picking out colors that show up nicely on the note paper you have chosen. Dark ink looks great on light paper colors and is very easy to read, especially for grandparents, who may have difficulty otherwise. A difficult combination, for example, would be light purple ink on orange paper. The colors blend too easily.

4. Stamps:

Your post office has an endless, wonderful variety of commemorative stamps to choose from. You can add a decorative touch to your envelopes by choosing these stamps. Commemorative stamps are specially designed to honor people, places, things (such as flowers and animals), special events, or occasions. They are the same price as regular First Class postage stamps. All you have to do is ask for them.

And be sure to buy enough stamps. The U.S. Postal Service prints a limited amount of each commemorative stamp. New designs are issued throughout the year. These stamps give you another opportunity to add FUN and an artistic touch to writing your Thank-You Notes. Enjoy picking out your favorites.

5. **Address File or Book:**
   There are many different ways of keeping track of names, addresses, and phone numbers. For example, some people use address books. Others use day planners, Rolodex® files, computers, etc. I use a recipe card file box that holds 4″ x 6″ cards, with alphabetical tabs. Later in this chapter, I will show you how I set up my own address card file.

6. **A Calendar:**
   A calendar helps to organize those special events that you need to know about *in advance,* such as birthdays to celebrate and the traditional holidays (i.e., Christmas and Hanukkah). It's on days like these that many people give and receive presents from both near and far. *Mark your calendar* about two weeks **in advance** of these occasions to remind yourself to check on your writing supplies.

*Do you have enough stationery **and** stamps?*

7. A Dictionary:

A Dictionary is a **must** when you need to look up the spelling of a word or its definition. After writing your first rough draft on scratch paper, always check your spelling. Make the necessary corrections *on the scratch paper* **before** copying the Thank-You Note onto your good stationery.

8. A Thesaurus:

A Thesaurus isn't a grammatical dinosaur. It is a very helpful reference book that gives lists of words that have basically the same meaning (also known as *synonyms*). You can choose the word that says exactly what you mean to say, such as:

The word *"note"* **could also be a:**
letter, missive, acknowledgment, reminder, or memo ...

When you feel *"happy,"* **you could also say you're:**
glad, delighted, or thrilled ...

A *"gift"* **may also be a:**
present, donation, favor, or contribution ...

"Wonderful" **can also be described as:**
great, extraordinary, amazing, fantastic, or marvelous ...

But why would you need a Thesaurus? Because it helps you find that special word, whether it is an adjective, noun, or verb, that truly expresses your feelings. You will discover a variety of new, helpful words when you start to explore the world through the "eyes" of a Thesaurus.

And Now ...

The Secret Key Ingredients For Having FUN!

9. Imagination:
This is secret key ingredient #1. When you use your imagination, you can be anyone, be anywhere you want to be, and be able to do some absolutely marvelous things. You'll be surprised what a little imagination can do to excite your creativity while composing a Thank-You Note, and with ...

10. A Good Sense of Humor:
This is secret key ingredient #2. By blending imagination, a good sense of humor, and of course, the specific details, you'll hear laughter even from faraway. *These two secret key ingredients are the FUN factors of the creative writing process.*

Setting Up Cat's Address Card File

The following are the supplies to set up a very flexible address file system:

1. Card Box (4" x 6")
This box can be plastic, pressed cardboard, metal, or wood. I use a plastic recipe box. You can even use a shoe box that can hold 4" x 6" cards, especially if you need extra storage space.

2. Index Cards (4" x 6")
These cards come in colors, such as white, blue, green, etc. Pick the color you like the best, or you can use one color for relatives and another for friends.

3. Index Dividers (4" x 6")
The dividers should have the letters of the alphabet, not numbers.

The information on each card should include:

1. The family (last) NAME located in the top left corner of the card. It is used when alphabetizing the cards.

2. The names of the individual family members living at the SAME address.

3. Phone numbers:
   Home, office, and fax *if available*

4. Birthday and Anniversary Dates

5. Address with the Zip Code
   (e-mail address if available)

6. You can also make any additional notes, such as their relationship to you, things they like to do, favorite colors, etc.

Let's take a look at the examples on the next page and see how you can set up your own file cards.

Cat's Address Card Format
actual size = 4" x 6"

LAST NAME	HOME PHONE # *(with area code)*
(in CAPITAL letters)	WORK PHONE # *(with area code)*

First Names	Birthday	Anniversary

Street Address

City, State, Zip Code

DOE	(H) (305) 555-1234
	(W) (305) 555-8989

	Birthday	Anniversary
John	11/2/51	6/15/76
Mary	12/6/51	
Jimmy	9/16/79	
Melissa	6/3/83	

246 Main Street

Any City, State 33000

One Box Can Hold Everything

Most Thank-You Note cards measure about 4" x 5," the perfect size to keep in the back of this type of address file, along with a supply of stamps, and a couple of pens. This way, all of your Thank-You Note writing supplies are in one neat little box.

This card file can be used for many other things, too. For example, when you want to put together a holiday card list or a guest list for a party, just pull out the cards you need and make a neat stack.

Whenever I send a greeting card, I make a note on the back of the file card to keep a record. I use abbreviations or symbols plus the last two digits of the year, such as **SG93** for *Seasons Greetings 1993.*

The following list shows the abbreviations I use:

Holidays Abbreviations

NY = Happy New Year
♥heart = Valentine's Day
♣shamrock = St. Patrick's Day
↶arching arrow over date = Passover
E = Easter
MD = Mother's Day
FD = Father's Day
GD = Grandparents Day
(Jewish New Year Date) 5756 = Rosh Hashanah
H = Halloween
TH = Thanksgiving
SG = Seasons Greetings
HAN = Hanukkah
XMAS = Christmas
KWNZ = Kwanzaa

Personal Abbreviations

BD = Birthday
BAR/M, BAT/M = Bar Mitzvah, Bat Mitzvah
CONF = Confirmation
QUIN = Quince
GRAD = Graduation
NJOB = New Job
ENG = Engagement
WED = Wedding*
AN = Anniversary
BABY = New Baby*
GW = Get Well
RET = Retirement
SYM = Sympathy, Condolences*

Be sure to update the file card for these additions or changes.

You can invent your own abbreviations. Be creative. Just make them quick and easy to remember. If a friend moves, fill out a new card and staple it to the front of the old address card. This will keep all of your correspondence code history intact on the back.

The "Write" Stuff

Gather together all of your writing materials and gift cards (with the gift's description on the back). A stack of cards is easier to handle than a pile of gift boxes. It streamlines the process by focusing your attention on writing your Thank-You Notes.

Find a Quiet Spot

Get comfortable and focus
      your thoughts on what
            you're going to write about
                  ***before** you start to write.*

CHAPTER THREE

LET'S SOLVE...

"The Mystery of The Unwritten Thank-You Note"

Tracking Down the Facts!

Good detectives know it's important to get *all* the facts. By knowing these details, your creativity will have a solid foundation on which to build (or should I say to "write") a Thank-You Note. Start by answering the following questions— The WHO?, The WHAT?, The WHY?, The WHEN?, and The HOW?:

1. "WHO gave you the Gift?"

    A Relative ...

    A Friend ...

    A Business Associate ...

2. "WHAT was the Gift? Is it ..."

Something you can wear?
A sweater ...
A shirt ...
A dress ...

Supplies for a hobby?
A model to be built ...
A computer game ...
An artist's box full of paints and brushes ...

Sporting Goods?
A bicycle helmet ...
A tennis racket ...
Skates, or running shoes ...

Perhaps ...
A Book?
A CD?
Tickets to a play or concert?
Dinner at a favorite restaurant?
A gift certificate?
A savings bond?
Money, or a check?

The list is endless.

3. "WHY did you receive the Gift?"

Birthday ...
Holiday ...
Special occasion ...
Get Well ...

4. "WHEN did you receive the Gift?"

At a birthday party ...
Christmas Eve ...
While you were home with the chicken pox ...

5. "HOW will you use the Gift?"

A check that could help pay for a CD player ...
A gift certificate to buy clothes ...
A baseball bat for hitting home runs ...

You get the idea!

But That's Not All There Is, Is It?

There are a few more details that can be useful. Now is the time to take another moment and think about any additional background information about the person who gave the present to you. These thoughts help develop creative elements that draw the reader into a closer personal relationship with the Thank-You Note writer. In my business we call it *"Human Interest"*—those little specific details that give writing a special, magical touch, such as:

Jeannie has been my friend since we were three years old and she lives with her family in Massachusetts.*

Grandma lives in another state and is an avid baseball fan ...

Aunt Mary is a pilot for a national airline and builds remote controlled aircraft in her spare time ...

Bob Smith is your Dad's business partner and a board member of the local Performing Arts Guild ...

Dr. Faith Walsh, a retired neurologist, is a beloved grandmother, an aspiring water colorist, and environmentalist ...*

Grandpa Jer is a ham radio operator and loves computers ...*

Jackie Eigen, was an ecology club member and newspaper recycler when we lived in the same college dormitory at the University of Miami in Florida. (I met my husband when he came over to drop off some newspapers at her place back in 1972.)*

*Ann Taylor, Past Employee Relations Manager for a
major insurance company, is an aspiring writer and
is one of my mentors...**

*Maryanne Schuessler Freeman, Past Associate Director
of Broadcast Operations for a Major TV Network,
is a business associate and long-distance pen pal ...**

*These are some of the very important people in my life.

I've given you a lot to think about here, but remember,
you ***don't*** have to use *every* last little detail.

> **Check out the Thank-You Note examples I've written in
> Chapters 8 and 9. The facts are listed on the left followed
> by a sample note on the right.**

That Makes "Sense"—
The <u>More</u> Perceptions The Better

Put your five senses to work:

SIGHT

SMELL

TASTE

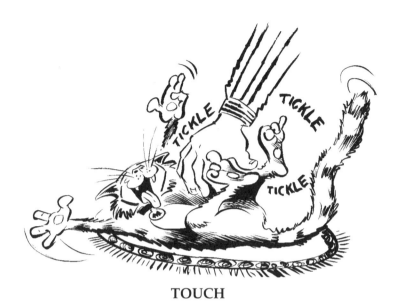

TOUCH

HEARING

Tune in your senses and become aware of an amazing amount of information. They can help you compose a more accurate description of the gift you received or the special event you attended (such as a party or concert performance).

And don't forget about your feelings. You can also describe how you felt about the gift, occasion, or function (such as happy or delighted). If you went to a function with a friend, relative, or associate, think about the conversations you had during or after the event. By using your senses you can more easily describe your impressions and feelings, then put those thoughts on paper.

A Quick Review of What to Do

1. Start by reviewing the specific details about the gift, the gift giver, the occasion, *and* your feelings.

2. Add a dash of imagination, and

3. Stir in a touch of humor.

What have you got? You have magically found all the special ingredients that make up "Cat's Creative Catalyst," which you will learn about in the next chapter. It's surprisingly easy to activate "Cat's Creative Catalyst." Take one word at a time, build a sentence at a time, and voilá, your Thank-You Note is done!

ALWAYS REMEMBER:
You will only be writing ONE Note At A Time!

CHAPTER FOUR

"CAT'S CREATIVE CATALYST"

What Is a "Creative Catalyst"?

Catalyst is a chemistry term. It's a substance that increases the rate of a chemical reaction without being changed or used up in the process. In our case, *creativity is a natural catalyst* that each of us has, which can be used to improve the Thank-You Note writing process. Creativity is located between the ears, behind the eyes, and encased in your imagination. Its effects are demonstrated every day in many ways.

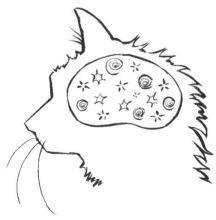

"Creative Catalyst" At Work

One of the reasons people come to me for help on their writing projects is because they know what they want to say, but they don't know HOW to say it! Many times people get stuck and confused, then become extremely frustrated after starting a Thank-You Note like this:

> *"Thank you for the _____."*
> (Filling in the blank with the gift)

I am known for having a "way with words." Along with the secret ingredients of *Imagination* and a *Good Sense of Humor*, and a little practice using your *"Creative Catalyst,"* you, too, will develop your own "way with words."

✳Here's How to Trigger Your Own "Creative Catalyst" and Write a Fantastic Note

1. *Think about how you felt when you received the gift.*
It helps to remember and picture in your mind what you were feeling as you opened the present, and what your initial reaction was. Describing these feelings are particularly helpful, especially if the gift giver wasn't there to share in the moment with you.

2. *Think about how you are going to use the gift.*
Be specific in your description of the gift and what you are planning to do with it.

3. *Think of something fun to say about the gift itself.*
This is where your imagination and sense of humor can add tremendous sparkle to your Thank-You Note.

4. *Then finish the note with the actual thank you.*
Include the person's name and a compliment, or comment as to when you will see the person in the future.

When you combine all of these, you have the ingredients to whip up a fantastic Thank-You Note that will absolutely delight and make the gift giver's day! *Remember: A sincere compliment always makes the gift giver feel especially good.*

Let's Take the Following Information and Add "Cat's Creative Catalyst"!

THE FACTS:

Aunt Nancy is your Mom's sister and she lives and works near Washington, D.C. She is a professional photographer and president of her own company. She has sent a personalized name plate to you for your desk for your birthday. Your Mom had recently taken you to visit her own office, and you liked many of the things she had on her desk.

THE NOTE:

> *street address*
> *city, state, Zip Code*
> *date*

Dear Aunt Nancy,
    You can't imagine how surprised I was when I opened your gift. I have been wanting a personalized name plate of my own ever since I visited Mom at work and saw hers. It looks great on my desk! Now I just need to figure out what kind of business I want to start. Do you have any ideas?
    Thank you, Aunt Nancy, you always know the best gifts to give! See you in August when we come up to visit. I can't wait to explore Washington, D.C., with you and Mom.

> *With Love,*
> *(your signature)*

How Did "Cat's Creative Catalyst" Work?

1. The words, *"surprised"* and *"wanting"* are feeling words. The "wanting" began when you saw your Mom's personalized name plate on her desk at work.

2. *"It looks great on my desk!"* describes how you are going to use it.

3. The "feelings" grew into *"imagining"* what it would be like to start your own business and who would be better able to answer your questions than Aunt Nancy? As president of her own company, she might have an idea about a good business for someone your age. By asking her a question now, you have opened the lines of communication to hear from Aunt Nancy again—another writing opportunity for *both* of you.

   This act of common courtesy, of writing a personal and sincere Thank-You Note, adds to the relationship that you share.

4. The note closes with the *"thank you,"* Aunt Nancy's name, the compliment, a "see you soon" comment, the closing (With Love), and *your signature.*

Now, you may be wondering how Aunt Nancy knew about your desire for a personalized name plate for your desk. I wouldn't be surprised if, when Aunt Nancy asked your Mom what you would like for your birthday, your Mom remembered your reaction to the visit to her office.

Creating A "Wish List"

When I worked at WPBT/Channel Two (the Public Television station in Miami, Florida), from 1974 to 1981, one of my friends was Anneke, who was born and raised in the Netherlands. She shared a family tradition with me and told me about creating "Wish Lists" and how her family would post them on the refrigerator. Since then, my family loves to put together "Wish Lists."

These lists can include anything, from a 40-foot sailboat to a baseball glove or an Arabian horse to surfboard wax. Of course, over the years the lists change, with items getting crossed off and new ones added. A "Wish List" allows a gift giver a wide choice as to what to get you, while knowing the gift selected will be something you would like to have.

CHAPTER FIVE

WHAT IF?
Other Items to Consider

What if ... you don't like the gift?

Every once in a while you might receive a gift you don't like. You might be disappointed, but those feelings do not belong in the Thank-You Note. The Thank-You Note is an acknowledgment of receiving the gift and the thoughtfulness on the part of the gift giver.

> **Focus on the positive aspects of the gift, the gift giver, and the occasion.**

What if ... you don't know the person who sent the gift?

There may be a special occasion such as a Bar Mitzvah or Confirmation where you might receive a gift from a business associate of your parents or from a distant relative you have never met before.

> **Ask your parents or another relative who the person is and what his or her relationship is to you, if any.**

For example: Mr. and Mrs. Woodcock, as well as Mr. and Mrs. Stevens, went to college with your parents; Aunt Esther is your father's aunt on his mother's side of the family, in other words, she would be your Great Aunt Esther.

What if ... you are concerned that you might say the wrong thing and hurt the person's feelings?

When you focus on the positive, and are sincere when you write a Thank-You Note, there is little chance of hurting someone's feelings.

They will be more hurt if you <u>don't</u> write the Thank-You Note.

What if ... you've already said "Thank You" in person or over the phone. Do you still need to write a Thank-You Note?

Yes. It's natural to respond with a verbal "Thank You." In fact, you may even say "*Why* ... THANK YOU!" when a gift is handed to you. And while the telephone is a handy way to communicate, it should not be used as a substitute for a written Thank-You Note.

A personal, handwritten note is still the <u>best</u> way to say "Thank You" for any gift you have received.

WATCH OUT! SOMETHING *FANTASTIC* IS ABOUT TO HAPPEN!

Let's Write The First Rough Draft

Whenever you start any project, thinking and planning will save you time, *every* time! Activate your own *"Creative Catalyst"* **before** you start to write. Think of your Thank-You Note as a three- to five-sentence way to easily and conveniently convey your heartfelt feelings to the person who sent the gift.

Your First Rough Draft is the playground where your creative thoughts can safely do cartwheels. As you think Thank-You Note thoughts, the words will begin to flow onto your scratch paper. However, don't limit yourself to just a few sentences. If you get on a roll, don't stop there. GO FOR IT! FULL SPEED AHEAD!

For those of you who wish to draft your Thank-You Note on your computer, go right ahead. However, after doing so, please rewrite the completed note onto your favorite stationery for that personal touch.

Use the following tools and techniques while writing your First Rough Draft:

1. Always **USE** the Dictionary to check your spelling, or your automatic spell checking program on your computer.

   Just remember though, your computer won't catch or "see" the difference between *homonyms*—words that sound the same, but are spelled differently, such as their, there, and they're.

2. Use the Thesaurus and discover new adjectives, nouns, and verbs.

3. Read your First Rough Draft aloud. This helps you make sure that the words flow smoothly. It makes it easier to find any grammatical errors, too.

4. Make any changes on the First Rough Draft.

> *Remember: You can always take a second piece of scratch paper and rewrite your First Rough Draft. This Second Draft may take a few minutes longer to do, but it will make it easier for you to read aloud and to copy onto your good stationery.*

5. If you are not quite satisfied with the way your note sounds, or if you haven't quite written what you wanted to say, set it aside for awhile and return to it later. More creative thoughts can emerge during this "resting period." Don't rush a piece of creative writing ... even if it is just a three- to five-sentence Thank-You Note.

The Layout of a Thank-You Note

A Thank-You Note consists of five basic parts and they include:

1. Your *address* and the *date* you are writing the letter in the upper right-hand corner,

2. The *greeting* or "salutation"—the most common one is "Dear _____,"

3. The *body of the note,*

4. The *closing,*—which could be "Love," or "Sincerely," or "Yours truly,"—and, of course,

5. Your *signature.* You can also put your phone number below your signature.

I wrote *"Why* ... THANK YOU!" to help you with the most important and biggest part, which is the **body of the note.** The following format is what I learned to use when I was a student.

```
                                    street address
                                    city, state, Zip Code
                                    date
    greeting

            body of the note

                                    closing

                                    signature
                                    phone number—optional
```

Here is a note using this format:

address & date
1000 Main Street
Pembroke Hills, FL 33000-1234
October 4, 1996

greeting
Dear Aunt Goldanna,

body of the note

When you said you had a surprise for me, I never expected it to be an engraved toothbrush holder. But I should have known, as one of my favorite aunts who just happens to be one of the longest practicing dentists in the state of New Jersey, you knew that I would really appreciate your gift. After all, I am a dentist's daughter, and besides you, I also have Uncle Max and Uncle Arthur. I'm surrounded by dentists.

Thank you, Aunt Goldanna. Your gift will be put to good use holding my favorite toothbrush whenever I go on a trip.

closing

Lots of Love,
Cat **signature**
(954) 555-0000

> *Be sure to include your last name whenever you send a note to someone other than a close relative or friend.*

Rewrite Your Note Carefully

Take your time when you rewrite your Thank-You Note. Do it *NEATLY* on your good stationery.

After you finish writing the note and addressing the accompanying envelope, put the date on the back of the gift card next to the gift's description and move it over to your "DONE" pile. Some people like to save the gift card, others just throw it away after writing the Thank-You Note.

Remember, sometimes grown-ups may want to know *if* you have written a particular Thank-You Note yet.

By checking the "DONE" date on the back of the gift card, you can tell them *exactly* when you did it.

How to Address the Envelope

On the front of the envelope, your home address goes in the upper left-hand corner, while the stamp goes in the upper right-hand corner. Your home address is also known as the *return address*. This allows the post office to return your note if they can't deliver it to the person to whom you have written.

The full name of the person you are sending the note to goes in the middle of the envelope along with their street address, city, state, and zip code. This person is also known as the *addressee*. You can see this illustrated on the next page.

return address
Cat Wagman
1000 Main Street
Pembroke Hills, FL 33000-1234

addressee
Goldanna Perlsweig, D.D.S.
123 Any Street
Somewhere, N.J. 98765-4321

Now all there is left to do is take your Thank-You Note to the post office and **mail it!**

When sending mail <u>*out of*</u> *the United States, write USA in capital letters below the Zip Code of your home (return) address.*

CHAPTER SEVEN

GETTING SERIOUS ABOUT THE SILLIES

A Few Words About SILLIES vs. SERIOUSLIES

Many people take writing *too seriously*. They frown, and wrinkle lines streak across their foreheads. They grind their teeth so much that they get horrible headaches. They end up tense all over with a bad case of the Seriouslies. No wonder they aren't in the mood to write anything.

My hope and desire is that everyone will have FUN while writing a Thank-You Note. So if you start to tense up, it's time for some Sillies.

Sillies are a great way to relax or change a tense or unhappy mood. The best way to do Sillies is to stand in front of a mirror and make funny faces. Of course, I use my own "Creative Catalyst Silly Sensor" whenever I need to improve my spirits!

The Sillier the Better!

Of course, you can do this by yourself or you can ask your parents to watch. If your parents need some Sillies, you can always get them started. You may even find out that your parents have some Sillies of their own that they might want to share with you.

The whole point of these Sillies is to help each of you to relax and get into the mood to enjoy the creative writing process.

CHAPTER EIGHT

KID NOTE EXAMPLES

The following chapter contains notes that will give you ideas on a variety of gifts and occasions. These examples are only my interpretations of how the facts can be used to write each note. Someone else may look at the same facts and come up with a completely different note—one that reflects his or her own point of view.

Why? Because it is how you apply your own *Imagination, Good Sense of Humor,* and *"Creative Catalyst"* that will make each note unique. *It's your voice,* not mine, *that you want to hear when you read your note aloud.*

I've included ten examples. For easy reading, I have placed facts on the left page and the corresponding note on the right.

THE FACTS:

For your birthday, you received a matching Chicago Cubs baseball cap and jacket with your name embroidered over the front pocket from your Grandma, who lives in Chicago. Your parents are going to let you visit her by yourself for the first time, during summer vacation.

THE NOTE:

street address

city, state, Zip Code

date

Dear Grandma,

Thanks for the great Chicago Cubs baseball cap and matching jacket. I really like having my name above the front pocket.

When you meet me at the gate, you'll be able to pick me out of the crowd when I get off the plane this summer. I will be properly suited up in my Birthday baseball cap and jacket.

I can't wait until we go to our first game this season. Love you, Grandma. I'll see you on the Fourth of July.

Love,

Joey

THE FACTS:

Cousin Brenda, who lives in New Jersey, sent a check for $100 for Devin's 10th birthday. With a check that large, Devin plans to put part of his gift money into his savings account; the rest he is going to spend on a radio-controlled car. In this case, $50 went into savings.

THE NOTE:

street address

city, state, Zip Code

date

Dear Cousin Brenda,

I decided to put part of your gift into my savings account, because some day I want to buy a real car. Today Dad is going to take me to the hobby shop so I can pick out the radio-controlled car I've wanted since I saw it six weeks ago. I can't wait to practice driving around the neighborhood by myself!

Thank you, Brenda, for such a generous gift. We're planning to be in New Jersey for two weeks in August. I'll be sure to pack my radio-controlled car, so you can try driving it, too. See you soon!

Love,

Devin

THE FACTS:

You receive an unexpected gift from your father's uncle George, (your great uncle), in honor of your graduation. The gift is an antique gold pocket watch that belonged to your great-grandfather. He included a letter telling the reason why your great-grandfather had been given the watch as a gift when he graduated from high school, too. At 85, Uncle George couldn't make it to the graduation ceremony, because he lives across the country and can't travel far from home.

THE NOTE:

> *street address*
> *city, state, Zip Code*
> *date*

Dear Uncle George,

   Though you were not able to attend my graduation, I know your thoughts and best wishes were with me.

   The note you sent telling how Great-Granddad had received the pocket watch as a high school graduation gift made me smile. I didn't know that he had a habit of being late for school, just like me. I can understand why his father wanted to be sure that Great-Granddad got to work on time every day, too, just like my Dad. The watch's chime sure sounds a lot better than my clock radio early in the morning!

   Thank you, Uncle George, for the antique gold watch and its incredible legacy. I'll be proud to carry on the family tradition of promptness. Take care and be well.

> *Sincerely,*
> *Mark*

THE FACTS:

For your birthday you received a complete anthology of the Sherlock Holmes mysteries by Sir Arthur Conan Doyle and a subscription to *Writer's Digest* magazine from your friend, Sharon, who also likes mysteries and knows that you want to become a mystery writer yourself.

THE NOTE:

street address

city, state, Zip Code

date

Dear Sherlock—I mean, Sharon,

I wonder how you figured out what I wanted for my birthday? Did I drop you a clue by making you read my latest mystery short story? Or perhaps, when we went to the book store together, you saw me flip through last month's Writer's Digest? *Or was it my comment about wanting to find one book with all of the Sherlock Holmes mysteries?*

Hmmmmm?

This note is elementary, my dear Sharon. It's a great big THANK YOU to an excellent detective and mystery-solving companion. Sir Arthur Conan Doyle would be proud of you!

Yours truly,

Ann

THE FACTS:

At Christmas you received a gift certificate for horseback riding lessons from your cousin, Meridith, who is a champion rider and jumper. The lessons will be given at Mountainside Stables, where Meridith keeps her own horse, Pegasus.

THE NOTE:

street address

city, state, Zip Code

date

Dear Cousin Meridith,

I jumped for joy this morning when I saw the horse design wrapping paper around my Christmas gift. From the size of the box though, I thought it had to be bigger than riding boots, but smaller than a saddle. When I opened your gift, I realized it was just the right size box for lots of fun and hours of enjoyment.

Thank you, Meridith, for sharing your love of horseback riding and for the gift certificate for the lessons at Mountainside Stables. I know that it will take lots of hard work and practice, but I hope, someday, to compete in the State Championships, too! Thank you again for making my birthday a blue-ribbon winner of a day!

Sincerely yours,

Colleen

THE FACTS:

For your birthday (in October), your Uncle Neil has given you a computer-designed certificate for tickets to a concert to be given by your favorite performer, who happens to be one of his favorites, too. He is going to take you out to dinner as well. Uncle Neil lives near the city where the concert is going to be held, and he plans to take you to it when your family comes up to visit during Thanksgiving vacation.

THE NOTE:

street address

city, state, Zip Code

date

Dear Uncle Neil,

I can't wait for Thanksgiving this year, because "Mr. Christopher" himself will be playing his fantastic saxophone at the Center of Performing Arts. Just think, six more weeks and you and I will be there, center row orchestra! What a day that Saturday will be, with the jazz concert and dinner, too!!

Thanks, Uncle Neil, I'm really looking forward to spending the day with you. This is one of my best Birthday presents ever.

Yours truly,

Greg

In this case, it would be appropriate to send another Thank-You Note after Thanksgiving. In it you can talk about the actual performance—mentioning certain songs or solos, and perhaps items about the restaurant—such as the delicious dessert, etc.

THE FACTS:

Aunt Martha, Grandma's sister, who always expects a Thank-You Note *by return mail*, has given you, the Bar Mitzvah Boy (Bat Mitzvah Girl), an expensive fountain pen—a family tradition. Your Dad still has his, the one he received from Aunt Martha, when he had his Bar Mitzvah. He showed you how to take care of yours so it will last a long time, too.

THE NOTE:

street address

city, state, Zip Code

date

Dear Aunt Martha,

You are the first one that I am writing to with the fabulous fountain pen that you gave me in honor of my becoming a Bar (Bat) Mitzvah. In fact, ALL of my Thank-You Notes will have that sophisticated "grown-up" look, thanks to you.

Dad showed me how to refill it without getting the ink all over me or on my desk. He also explained how to store it properly and to write a "squiggle" on a piece of scratch paper first to make sure the ink is flowing smoothly.

I'm glad you were able to share this special time with my family and me. Thank you, again, Aunt Martha, for the great fountain pen!

Love,

Joshua (Anna)

P.S. I'm going to let the ink dry first, though, before I drop this in the mail.

P.S. or postscript *is a little afterthought that is added to a note below your signature.*

THE FACTS:

As co-captain of your basketball team, you are known for your three-point long shots. During practice, while going up for a corner shot, one of your opponents tried to block you and you ended up injuring your knee and ankle. As a result, you were in the hospital and missed the county play-offs. After you got home, the team showed up and gave you the game ball with all of their signatures. As an extra surprise, Coach Walsh gave a copy of the videotape Mrs. Alexander (one of the parents) had shot during the game to you.

THE NOTE:

street address

city, state, Zip Code

date

Dear Coach Walsh and the Morristown Colonials,

You know how disappointed I was about getting injured during practice right before the county play-offs. You and the entire team are more than just the county champs—you're the best medicine I could hope for.

When the whole team came by yesterday and crowded into my room, I couldn't believe it! I couldn't stay miserable with all that excitement going on. Please thank everyone for cheering me up. The autographed game ball is great, and Mrs. Alexander did an excellent job with the videotape, too.

I plan to be in Trenton for the State Championships to cheer everyone onto another winning season. You're already winners in my book. Thanks again, Coach, for helping me get through this "unintentional benching."

Gratefully yours,

Larry Dover

THE FACTS:

Your birthday falls on the 4th of July and you receive a jogging suit from your Grandma Kate, who is an exercise "nut." At 72, she can run circles around some of your friends. Your Dad runs three miles every other day and you are thinking about going out for the track team next year.

THE NOTE:

street address

city, state, Zip Code

date

Dear Grandma Kate,

I had to laugh this morning when you ran over to my house to drop off my birthday gift and even more so, when you ran in place waiting for me to open it up. I should have known that it would have something to do with exercising!

Thank you, Grandma Kate, for the "patriotic" jogging suit. The red, white, and blue design will be a definite reminder of when I got the energetic boost in my running career. Dad is still running his three miles every other day, and I'm starting to run with him to get into shape for next year's track team. Keep up the good pace, Grandma—you're the greatest!

Love,

Michael

THE FACTS:

When you graduated from the University of Miami in Florida, your grandfather gave you a new sewing machine capable of doing all sorts of fancy stitches, because you love to sew. You recently moved into your own apartment, and have plenty of windows that need curtains, and a sofa that needs pillows. You also have a new job working at the Public Television Station, WPBT/Channel Two.

THE NOTE:

street address

city, state, Zip Code

date

Dearest Granddaddy,

   Your timing couldn't have been better. Now that I am in my own unfurnished apartment, I have plenty of ideas on how I want to decorate my new home. My apartment is not far from the University of Miami and only thirty minutes from my job at WPBT/Channel Two, the Public Television Station that serves South Florida.

   The fabulous sewing machine that you gave me as a graduation gift can do all sorts of neat things. I'll send you some pictures of my latest adventures in sewing later this month. Until then, thank you for your generous gift, Granddaddy. I can't wait to pick out the fabric for my new bedroom curtains and sofa pillows.

Love,

Cathy

CHAPTER NINE

GROWN-UP NOTE EXAMPLES

The following chapter contains notes written in appreciation of gifts, and for occasions that a grown-up may encounter. As I mentioned in Chapter Eight, "KID NOTE EXAMPLES," these examples are only my interpretations of how the facts can be used to write each note. Again remember, someone else may look at the same facts and come up with a completely different note.

Don't forget, it's how grown-ups apply their own *Imaginations*, *Good Senses of Humor*, and *"Creative Catalysts"* that will make each note unique. *It's their voices*, not mine, *that they want to hear when they read their notes aloud.*

The format in this chapter is the same as the previous Kid Notes' one. For easy reading, I have placed the facts on the left page and the corresponding note on the right.

THE FACTS:

For Christmas you received tickets for the musical, *A Chorus Line,* from Bob Smith, a business associate, and a "babysitter certificate" from his teenage daughter, Marggie, to watch your children while you and your spouse go the theatre. You have known Marggie since she was small.

In this case, two separate Thank-You Notes need to be written, one to Bob and one to Marggie, and mailed separately.

NOTE #1:

street address

city, state, Zip Code

date

Dear Bob,

Just a quick note to thank you for the theatre tickets you sent us. My wife and I are thrilled at the opportunity to spend an evening alone together enjoying A Chorus Line. *When the applause raises the roof at the end of this hit Broadway show, just know that part of the applause is for you and your generosity.*

Thanks again, Bob, for this special holiday gift.

Sincerely,

Richard Evans

Laurie Evans

NOTE #2:

> *street address*
> *city, state, Zip Code*
> *date*

Dear Marggie,

My wife and I were delighted to receive your special "Baby-sitter Certificate." We have known you since you were our own children's ages and have seen you grow into a mature young lady. Your gift certainly gives us the "peace of mind" knowing our children will be well taken care of while we go to see
A Chorus Line.

Thank you, Marggie, for helping to make a wonderful evening even better.

> *Sincerely,*
> *Richard Evans*
> *Laurie Evans*

THE FACTS:

Mrs. Szeeley, your girlfriend's mother you've known since you were in sixth grade, attended your bridal shower. The shower had a kitchen theme and she gave you a "Top of the Stove" bun warmer.

THE NOTE:

> *street address*
> *city, state, Zip Code*
> *date*

Dear Mrs. Szeeley,

What a wonderful addition to my kitchen collection! I still have memories of all the delicious food that you lovingly prepared for Pam and me, especially your homemade soup. YUM!

Thank you, Mrs. Szeeley, for the green bun warmer that you gave me as a bridal shower gift. It's so convenient to use, but Jan, my husband-to-be, is starting to wonder about me, and why I'm sitting on the stove all the time.

> *Sincerely yours,*
> *Cathy*

THE FACTS:

Aunt Carol and Uncle Jerry sent a wooden salad bowl set as a wedding gift. They purchased the gift at the kitchenware store where you had registered* for several items.

When a couple plans to get married, stores have special lists called Registries, where the couple can write down their requests for gifts. The gifts can include all sorts of items and objects, such as: kitchen appliances, china, silverware, glassware, towels, sheets, etc.

These are similar to the "Wish Lists" mentioned in Chapter 4.

THE NOTE:

street address

city, state, Zip Code

date

Dear Aunt Carol and Uncle Jerry,

How did you know that teak is our favorite kind of wood? Did a little "mother" bird tell you? The salad bowl set will definitely liven our dinner table, along with your company.

We would like to say "thank you" in person, too, so please accept our invitation to dinner for Saturday, June 13th, at six o'clock.

Love,

Johnny and Ellen

R.S.V.P. by June 6th

(908) 555-1111

An R.S.V.P. *means* répondez s'il vous plaît. *It is a French phrase which asks a person to please reply to the invitation. When it is a formal invitation, such as a invitation to a wedding, there is usually a separate response card to be mailed back to the sender. For an invitation to a party, the sender may put an* R.S.V.P. *with a date and the telephone number to call below it. The* R.S.V.P. *call is made on or before this date to let the host or hostess know whether* <u>or not</u> *the guest is planning to attend.*

THE FACTS:

Next is a belated Thank-You Note I sent to my mother-in-law for a leather purse she gave me for my birthday. At the time the Environmental Protection Agency (EPA) was in the news and my husband owns a penknife.

THE NOTE:

> *street address*
>
> *city, state, Zip Code*
>
> *date*

Dear Rho,

Once upon a time there was this 30-year-old bump on a log, who just sat there, twiddling her twigs, watching the world float by. Now this bump knew she should get her trunk in gear, so she tapped her husband on the limb and asked if she could borrow his pen knife. Oh, so-o-o-o slowly and carefully, she carved the biggest THANK YOU the EPA would allow ...

Thank you, Rho, you have the best taste in clothes, accessories, and sons! I just <u>love</u> my new leather purse with all its pockets. Oh, and I finally got an excavation permit to clean out my old one, so the material transfer will be completed before you receive this note!

> *Love,*
>
> *Cat*

THE FACTS:

Ana Sanchez was responsible for securing a variety of corporate sponsors and donations for a local charity auction. The following is an example of a Thank-You Note she sent to Ms. Pauline Hope, CEO of the Hope Cookie Corporation. Each year Ms. Hope can be counted on to donate a unique container filled with her premium cookies. This year's donation was a beautiful antique cookie jar. The bidding was fast and enthusiastic when it reached the auction block.

THE NOTE:

street address

city, state, Zip Code

date

Dear Ms. Hope,

On behalf of our charity auction, I wanted to thank you for your delicious donation. Since you attended our auction, you are aware that when your antique cookie jar was put up for bid, everyone wanted to buy it. We were all delighted with the audience's response. Your and their generosity helped us to reach our goal of raising $25,000.

Thank you, again, Ms. Hope, we couldn't have done it without your continued support.

With Deepest Appreciation,

Ana Sanchez

THE FACTS:

You had a baby boy, Charlie, your second child, and you received a baby bag with many pockets from a friend who is in charge of a large department at work.

THE NOTE:

> *street address*
>
> *city, state, Zip Code*
>
> *date*

Dear Maryanne,

Thanks for the great baby bag. It has a place for everything that Charlie and I could possibly need whenever we go out. One question though—Where's the "third hand"?—that's something else I could **really** *use right about now!*

Thanks again, Maryanne. You **always** *manage to find ways to help me get better organized, especially now that I'm knee-deep in children!*

> *With Love,*
>
> *Susan*

THE FACTS:

Aunt Sylvia sent a collection of baby booties and a baby blanket for Aaron, your newborn son. The Thank-You Note is written from Aaron. (This is a good example of putting yourself in another person's place and writing from his or her point of view.)

THE NOTE:

street address

city, state, Zip Code

date

Dear Aunt Sylvia,

My Mom said it was your magic fingers that made the beautiful baby blanket and all of those booties, too, just for me. Now, my tootsies will be toasty seven days a week!

Thank you, Aunt Sylvia, for the handmade gifts. The Mom of my friend, Pete, wants to know if you can make some booties for him, too, because they are the first ones she has seen that I can't take off as fast as 1-2-3. Pete is always taking his off. He likes to chew on his tootsies, too.

Mommy and Daddy send their love. How do I look all wrapped up in the blanket? Daddy took the picture. Mommy says I've got Daddy's smile. Can't wait to meet you!

With Hugs and Kisses,

Aaron

When sending a photograph, use a non-smearing, quick-drying, permanent marker to write the names of the people, the date, and the occasion on the back. A clear adhesive label or tape can be placed over the information for additional protection.

THE FACTS:

When my son, Bernie, was in kindergarten, his teacher was Barbara Lenes. At the end of the year I sent the following note to her.

THE NOTE:

street address

city, state, Zip Code

date

Dear Barbara,

Thank you for helping to make Kindergarten such a positive experience for Bernie. With all of your patience, understanding, and LOVE, Bernie has achieved a lot this year. He's gotten a great start on the long road to his higher education.

Thank you, Barbara. You have made a great difference for all of our children. Because you care so much about them, you have encouraged them in all they can do and all that they can become.

With Sincerest Appreciation,

Cat Wagman

THE FACTS:

Aunt Meryl is famous for her baking ability and every Christmas Eve she would give us one of her magnificent Holiday Stollens. A Stollen is a sweet yeast bread filled with chopped fruits and nuts, and shaped in a long loaf.

THE NOTE:

street address

city, state, Zip Code

date

Dear Aunt Meryl,

The heavenly aroma of your Holiday Stollen still fills the house on this beautiful Christmas morning. The entire family always loves to share this traditional breakfast after opening their presents.

Of course, they made sure that I had it warming in the oven <u>before</u> *I could unwrap my first present. Everyone was smiling as they savored each tender, fruit-filled morsel.*

Thank you again, Aunt Meryl. Everything you bake has that down-home, comforting quality that warms our hearts on this cold, wintry morning in northern New Jersey. Have a Happy and Healthy New Year.

With Love,

Sarah

THE FACTS:

When I was preparing to give my first *"Why* ... THANK YOU!" note writing FUNshop™ to my son Devin's third grade class, I approached the main post office in Miami to see if they had any old commemorative stamp posters that they would be willing to give me. The clerk who was able to fill my request was named Simon.

THE NOTE:

street address

city, state, Zip Code

date

Dear Simon,

I would like to thank you for your assistance today in locating the postage stamp posters I needed for my Thank-You Note writing classes.

I thought I would only be able to find just one, but you were able to give me six!

Now, I just have to decide which ones to use in my son Devin's third grade class on Friday, May 11th. I know, I'll make it easy on myself and let him choose. Thanks again, Simon, the posters will make great visual aids for the class.

Sincerely,

Cat Wagman

CHAPTER TEN

CONDOLENCES

Thank-You Notes to Those Who Help You Get Through a Time of Sorrow

Death is part of everyday life. Whether it is expected or unexpected, it is still a shock and the sadness surrounding a death can be very deep—whether it's a relative, a friend, or a pet.

Many people will reach out to you to comfort you during this time of sorrow. They may visit you, send flowers, make a donation to a favorite charity, or any number of things to let you know that they care and understand what you are feeling. They want you to know that they are there to help you in any way they can.

Writing Thank-You Notes is the easiest way to let them know you appreciate their willingness and helpfulness, flowers, donations, and such. This is a rough time because your feelings of sadness are very strong.

When you write a Thank-You Note, do share your thoughts and appreciation for what they have done for you. Focus on a happy moment that you shared with the person who died, especially if you shared the moment with the person to whom you are writing the note.

A Personal Experience

To help illustrate this, I want to share a personal experience. In 1993 I was asked by my mother's family to express their feelings in a note after my grandfather died. The note on the following page is what I wrote on their behalf.

Although we had it printed on ivory-colored stationery, a personal note was *written* on the bottom or back of each card. We acknowledged everyone who helped us immediately after his death and who sent condolences, flowers, and made charitable donations in his honor.

The family of Dr. Israel J. Cramer
    mourns his passing.
He touched all our lives in so many ways—
    as a father, a doctor, and a teacher;
His steadfast love for his children,
    family, and friends;
His unwavering concern for and gentleness with
    his patients, and
His lifelong commitment to his Jewish heritage
    and legacy.
With Love, the memory of his kind words and
    unselfish giving of himself lives on.
Thank you for remembering him.

The following is a sample of another note, using the same format as in Chapters 8 and 9.

THE FACTS:

Phillip, a family acquaintance and childhood friend of Great-Grandma Rose, attended her funeral. He gave the family a framed photograph of Rose and himself taken when they were children. The picture captured a special moment when the two of them were fishing off a dock.

THE NOTE:

> *street address*
> *city, state, Zip Code*
> *date*

Dear Phillip,

The flood of emotions has begun to subside. Taking each new day, one at a time. All that is done, sits in the back of my mind. All that there is to do, must start somewhere.

As I sit here, the numbness of my loved one gone reflects my grief. You reached out. Your caring touched me. Your love held me. Your strength supported me—for that I am thankful.

Great-Grandma Rose always talked about you and how you taught her to fish when nobody else would. She's the one who taught me. Thank you, Phillip, for coming to say good-bye to Great-Grandma, and for the picture of the best fishing buddies in the world. I bet she's teaching the angels all your fishing tricks right now!

> *Truly yours,*
> *Beverly Raymond*

AFTERWORD

My Thank-You to You!

As a writer, I truly care about writing. I love to write. It's a love that can be shared with everyone, especially through something as simple as a Thank-You Note.

Many people haven't had a chance to learn how much FUN writing Thank-You Notes can be. Now, by thinking "Thank-You Note Thoughts" and using **your own** *"Creative Catalyst,"* writing any note can be FUN, quick, and easy to do. It has been a pleasure to share my Thank-You Note writing techniques and the tricks of my writing trade with you.

If you have *ever* played basketball and sank a 3-point shot **without** the ball touching the rim, you know how *great* that feels. But you also know that it takes hours of practice to achieve perfect shots and to play at that **level** with confidence. It's the same with writing, too. Writing is a craft that needs to be practiced every day. When you are having FUN and **ENJOY** what you are *doing*, it only gets better and better.

I hope that *"Why ...* THANK YOU!" will encourage you to explore other forms of creative writing, too. Who knows where your writing will lead you—perhaps, someday, you will become a professional writer, too!

Cat Wagman
June 13, 1996
Pembroke Pines, Florida

I'm a Curious "Cat," and
I Would Like to Know ...

What you think about this book? Did you find it helpful? Was it easy to understand? Would you drop me a note? I would love to hear from you.

If you know of someone or another group who you think would enjoy my book, or would like more information about my *Why* ... THANK YOU! FUNshops™, please *write* to me:

Cat Wagman
c/o Working Words, Inc.
1689 N. Hiatus Road, Suite 114
Pembroke Pines, FL 33026-2129

or via e-mail:

WhyThankU@aol.com

Index

References to illustrations are printed in italics.

ATTENTION!
SCHOOLS, CORPORATIONS,
AND
PROFESSIONAL ORGANIZATIONS

Quantity discounts are available on bulk purchases of this creative writing guide for educational training, fund raising, or gift giving. The author is also available to present *Why* ... THANK YOU! FUNshops™.

For more information contact:

Marketing Department
c/o Working Words, Inc.
1689 N. Hiatus Road, Suite 114
Pembroke Pines, FL 33026-2129

Or e-mail: WhyThankU@aol.com

Or call: 1-954-431-5597
Monday through Friday
10 a.m. to 4 p.m. EST

Join the Annual Celebration of
International Thank You Days ©**94/95/96**
January 11th through January 18th

For more information, please contact:
Adrienne Sioux Koopersmith
(773) 743-5341 • fax: (773) 743-5395
e-mail: kooper@interaccess.com

Why ... THANK YOU!

How to Have FUN Writing Fantastic Notes and More ...

Order Form

	Quantity	Price	Total
Paperback		@$12.95	
Printed Hard Cover		@$15.95	
		Subtotal	
		Florida residents add 6% sales tax	
		(see below) **Shipping**	
		(U.S. Funds) **TOTAL ENCLOSED**	$

CHECK/Money Order #: _____

Method of Payment: Checks or Money Orders in U.S. Funds only (payable to Working Words, Inc.)

Shipping Charges: U.S. destinations add $3.00 (or $3.50 for hard cover) for first book and $1.00 (or $1.50 for hard cover) for each additional book. All U.S. orders shipped Special Fourth Class Mail (Bookrate). Please allow three to four weeks delivery.

Please Type or Print NEATLY

Ship to:

Name: _____

Address: _____

_____

City: _____

State: _____ **Zip Code:** _____

Return this form to: Working Words, Inc.
2114 N. Flamingo Road, # 1114
Pembroke Pines, FL 33028-3501
www.ThankYouThankYou.com
For more information, please call (954) 431-5597
Mon-Fri, 10 a.m. to 4 p.m. EST

■ *c.* AD 1523 – 32 Spanish churches are built over Mexica sites.

Spanish overlords receiving tribute.

■ AD 1810 – 1821 Mexico breaks from Spain and becomes an independent country.

■ Present Over one million people speaking Nahuatl, the language of the Mexica, live in Central Mexico today.

Cathedral in Mexico City, built on the remains of Tenochtitlan.

■ *c.* 1521 – 1600 Most indigenous people are converted to Catholicism.

■ AD 1535 – 1821 The Spanish rule Mexico; many landowners exploit the labour of indigenous people.

■ *c.* AD 1650 The indigenous population recovers. A mestizo population of mixed indigenous and Spanish descent emerges.

Market day in Cuetzalan, State of Puebla. The majority of the local people are Nahuatl-speakers.